Four Fa Friends

WRITTEN BY DIANE STORTZ

ILLUSTRATED BY BILL DICKSON

ISBN 0-7847-1716-8

11 10 09 08 07 06   9 8 7 6 5 4 3 2

Standard®
PUBLISHING
Bringing The Word to Life

Cincinnati, Ohio

There was a man who couldn't walk who wanted to see Jesus. He wanted Jesus to make him well. But how would he get to the house where Jesus was?

The man's friends talked it over. "No problem!" they said.

And they carried him on his mat to the house where Jesus was.

But when they got there, they couldn't get in. There was no room inside the house, no room outside the house, no room anywhere—*except* on the roof.

"No problem!" said the four friends. And they carried the man up to the roof.

But now they had a problem. How would they get the man into the house to see Jesus?

"No problem!" they said. And they made a hole in the roof.

The people in the house looked up. They saw the four friends and the man on his mat. How *would* the man get down?

"No problem," said the friends. Slowly, they lowered the man on his mat through the hole in the roof, into the house where Jesus was.

No one talked. No one moved. Could Jesus heal a man who couldn't walk?

"No problem!" said the man's four friends.

Everyone was amazed and filled with wonder when the man stood up and picked up his mat. "We haven't seen anything like this before!" they said.

And the man walked out the door and went home, praising God because Jesus had healed him.